Insects All Around

by Margie Burton, Cathy French, and Tammy Jones

Table of Contents

What Is an Insect?

An insect has
six legs and
three body parts.

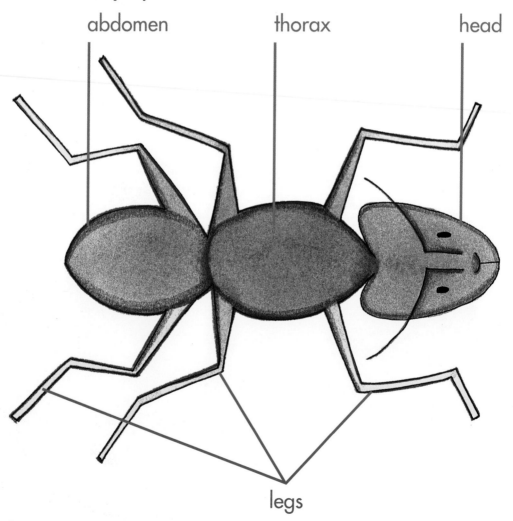

abdomen   thorax   head

legs

butterfly

These are all insects.

mosquito

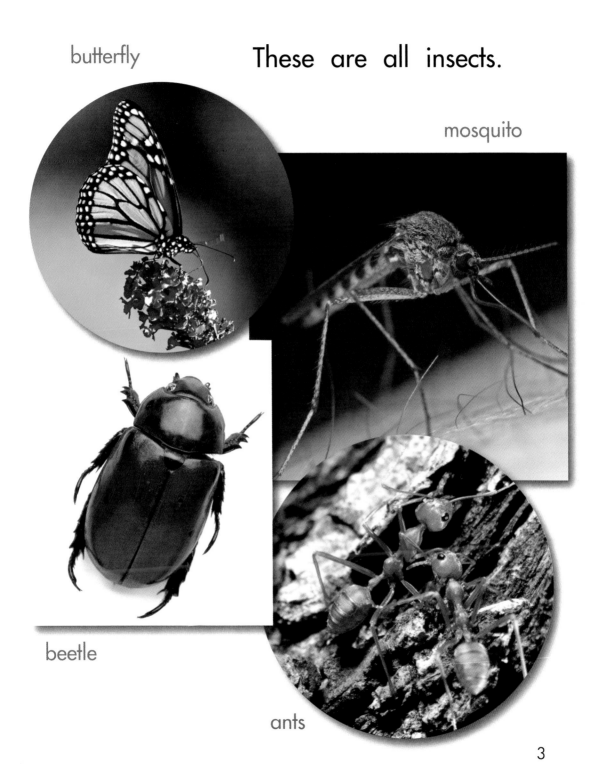

beetle

ants

What Does an Insect Look Like?

Many insects are very, very small. They are not even one inch long.

The smallest insects can go through the eye of this needle.

Some insects are big.

rhinoceros beetle

Some insects are more than
four inches long.

Many insects have antennae.
They use them to smell
and feel.

cockroach

Many insects have two eyes. They cannot move their eyes or see very far. Their eyes stay open all the time.

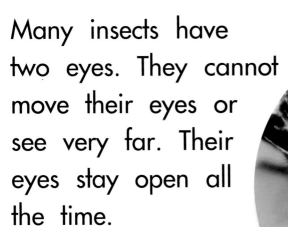

dragonfly

fly

7

Some insects make sounds.

cricket

cicada

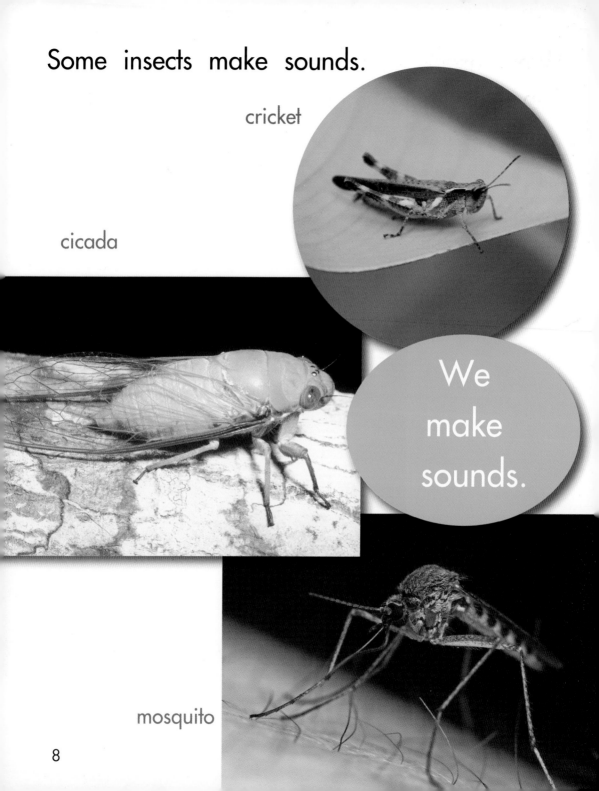

We make sounds.

mosquito

8

Many insects can hide.
Can you see the insects?

This insect
looks like
a stick.

walking stick

This insect
looks like a
green leaf.

grasshopper

What Can Insects Do?

Some insects can fly.

butterfly

ladybug

We can fly.

fly

wasp

Insects fly so that they can look for food. They also fly so that they can get away from animals.

Lizards eat insects.

Many animals eat insects.

Birds eat insects.

Frogs eat
insects, too.

How Can Insects Help?

Some insects can help the plants make seeds. Bees go from plant to plant getting sweet food. When they do this, they help to make new seeds.

bee

Bees also give us honey.

They take the sweet food back to the hive and make the honey.

How Can Insects Be Pests?

Some insects eat plants.

Beetles eat leaves.

Some insects bite us.

Mosquitoes bite us.

Some insects hurt our homes.

Termites hurt our homes.

Insects are all around us.